Epic Cars

Audi R8

MEGAN COOLEY PETERSON

I0886598

BLACK RABBIT BOOKS

Bolt is published by Black Rabbit Books
P.O. Box 3263, Mankato, Minnesota, 56002.
www.blackrabbitbooks.com
Copyright © 2021 Black Rabbit Books

Jen Besel, editor; Grant Gould, designer;
Omay Ayres, photo researcher

All rights reserved. No part of this book may be reproduced, stored in a retrieval system or transmitted in any form or by any means, electronic, mechanical, photocopying, recording, or otherwise, without written permission from the publisher.

Library of Congress Cataloging-in-Publication Data
Names: Peterson, Megan Cooley, author.
Title: Audi R8 / by Megan Cooley Peterson.
Description: Mankato, Minnesota : Black Rabbit Books, [2021] | Series: Bolt. Epic cars | Includes bibliographical references and index. | Audience: Ages 8-12 | Audience: Grades 4-6 | Summary: "Experience what it's like to be behind the wheel of an Audi R8 through exciting text, vibrant photography, and labeled images and other graphics"— Provided by publisher.
Identifiers: LCCN 2019027455 (print) | LCCN 2019027456 (ebook) | ISBN 9781623102548 (hardcover) | ISBN 9781644663509 (paperback) | ISBN 9781623103484 (ebook)
Subjects: LCSH: Audi R8 automobile (Racing automobile)—Juvenile literature.
Classification: LCC TL215.A825 P48 2021 (print) | LCC TL215.A825 (ebook) | DDC 629.222/2—dc23
LC record available at https://lccn.loc.gov/2019027455
LC ebook record available at https://lccn.loc.gov/2019027456

Printed in the United States. 4/20

Image Credits

audi-mediacenter.com: Audi MediaCenter, Cover (car), 4–5, 6 (t), 8–9, 11 (t), 12–13, 14–15 (t & b), 16–17, 19, 24 (car), 26, 27, 28–29, 31, 32; audi.com: Audi Sport, 1, 3; audiusa.com: Audi USA, 11 (b), 18–19, 21; caradvice.com.au: 22–23; cnet.com: Road Show, 6 (b); flickr.com: Mode Carbon, 11 (c); partsscore.com: Parts Score, 22 (inset); Shutterstock: Elenamiv, Cover (bkgd); GarikProst, 24 (t)

Every effort has been made to contact copyright holders for material reproduced in this book. Any omissions will be rectified in subsequent printings if notice is given to the publisher.

Contents

CHAPTER 1
Racing Down the Road. 4

CHAPTER 2
Design. 10

CHAPTER 3
Power and Performance. 20

CHAPTER 4
An Epic Car. 29

Other Resources. 30

CHAPTER 1

Racing Down the Road

The Audi R8's engine roars as it races down the road. The car sits low to the ground. Its smooth body shines. It has no trouble reaching almost 200 miles (322 kilometers) per hour.

R8 VS. R8 GT3 LMS

2019 R8 GT3 LMS

585
horsepower

STARTS AT
$460,000

2020 R8

562
horsepower

A New Update

Audi **unveiled** the original R8 in 2006. Each year, it updated and improved the car. Then, in 2018, the company released the updated R8 coupe. The new R8 shares more than 50 percent of its parts with the R8 GT3 LMS race car. The R8 is built for regular roads. But it has the power of a race car.

STARTS AT

$169,900

PARTS OF A 2019 AUDI R8

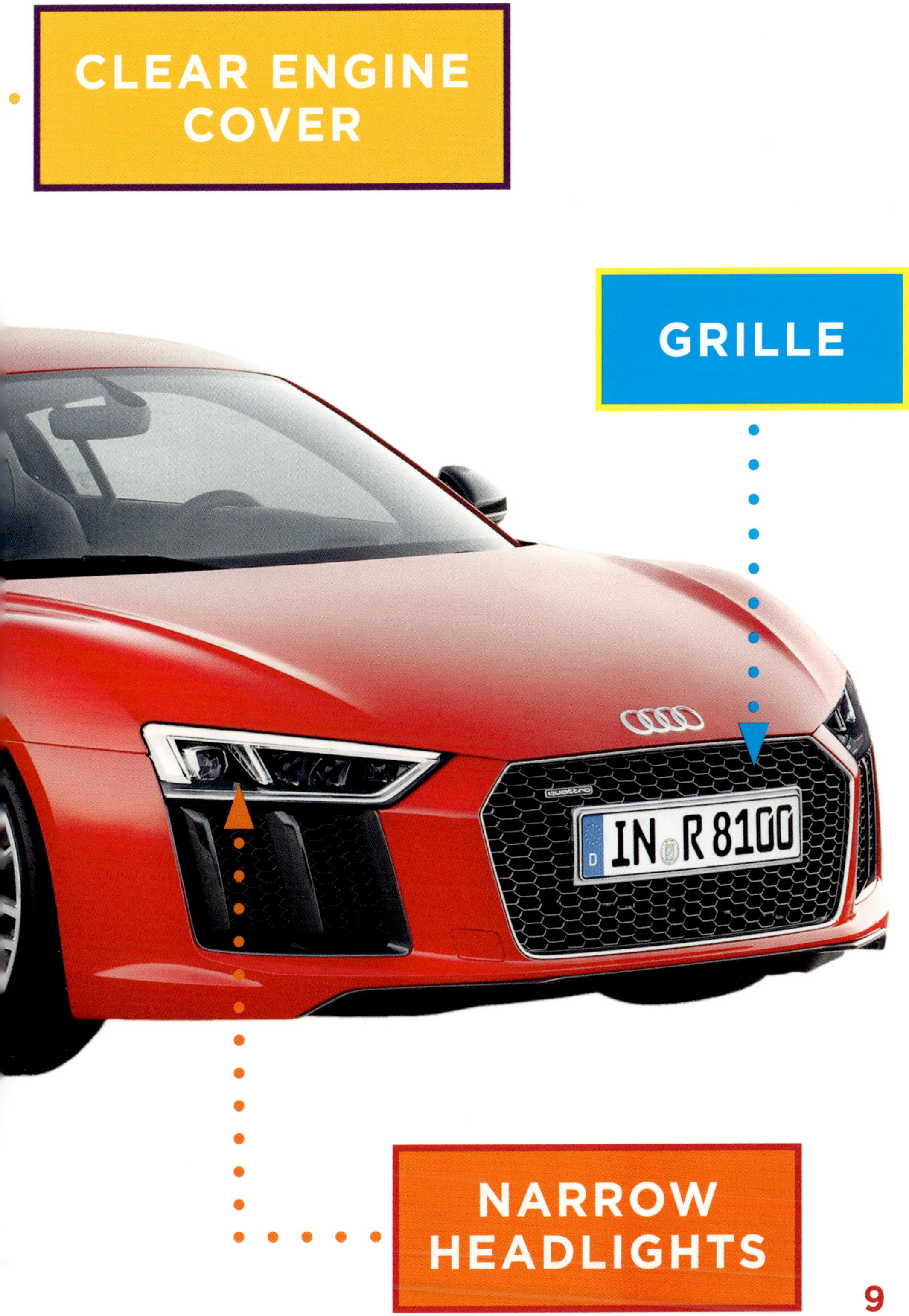
CLEAR ENGINE COVER
GRILLE
IN R 8100
NARROW HEADLIGHTS

CHAPTER 2

Design

The R8 begs to be looked at. **Carbon fiber** body panels keep the car light. A large front grille has a honeycomb pattern. The roof slopes toward the back. The engine is showcased under a clear cover.

CARBON FIBER BODY

GRILLE

ENGINE COVER

The R8 also comes in a convertible. The convertible is called the R8 Spyder.

All about Air

Engineers designed the R8 to be **aerodynamic**. Air passes easily through inlets at the front and back. The inlets reduce **drag**. Side inlets draw in air to cool the engine.

The Interior

The inside of the Audi R8 is classic and clean. Racing seats can be adjusted to 18 settings. The steering wheel is flat on the bottom to give drivers more legroom. The R8 has a digital dashboard that displays dials and **gauges**. The dashboard also shows maps and music.

RADIO IN
Rundenzeiten
Performance
snow
wet
dry
Verbrauch
VIEW
NAV
drive select
START ENGINE STOP
R
N
D/S

700km
Purple Rain In The...
Stammham
Hitzhofen
Adelschlag
Oberdolling
Kösching
Gaimersheim
Buxheim
Nassenfels
Dünzlau
Ingolstadt
Großmehring
Bergheim
Gerolfing
Ringsee
Schafirrsee
Hagau
Manching
Ernsgad
Forstwiesen
Pichler See
M3
1/min x 1000
50
km/h
370 m
B13
2,5 km
17:30
+21.0°C

THE COCKPIT

SPEAKERS
RACING SEATS

Personalized

Drivers can **customize** the R8 to fit their style. The car comes in 11 exterior colors. The wheels come in two sizes. The seats come in black, red, brown, and white leather.

Each R8 takes more than 70 hours to build.

CHAPTER 3

Power and Performance

The Audi R8 is all about speed. It comes with a powerful V10 engine. It has 562 horsepower. But buyers can choose the upgraded V10 Plus. That option gives them 602 horsepower. The upgraded car can go from 0 to 60 miles (97 km) per hour in 3.2 seconds.

COMPARING SPEEDS

2020 Audi R8 (with V10 Plus)

2019 Acura NSX

2019 DBS Superleggera

2018 Maserati GranTurismo MC

miles per hour

V10
FSI

205 (330 km)
191 (307 km)
211 (340 km)
187 (301 km)
160
170
180
190
200
210
220

Shock Absorbers

The R8 delivers a smooth ride at high speeds. The car's **shock absorbers** hold a **magnetic** liquid. This liquid adjusts the shock absorbers automatically. The all-wheel drive R8 can take corners quickly and still keep its balance.

DRIVING MODES

COMFORT

a soft, less bumpy ride

AUTO

automatically adjusts settings to the driver's handling

DYNAMIC

acts like a race car

INDIVIDUAL

lets drivers choose their own settings

PERFORMANCE

(on R8 V10 Plus models)

louder and more aggressive

Driving Modes

This car has a driving mode to fit every driver. Owners can change the mode whenever they want. The modes adjust the car's **suspension**, steering, and even engine noise.

By the Numbers

about **22** miles (35 km) per gallon

ESTIMATED HIGHWAY **MILEAGE**

$169,900

BASE PRICE OF THE 2020 MODEL

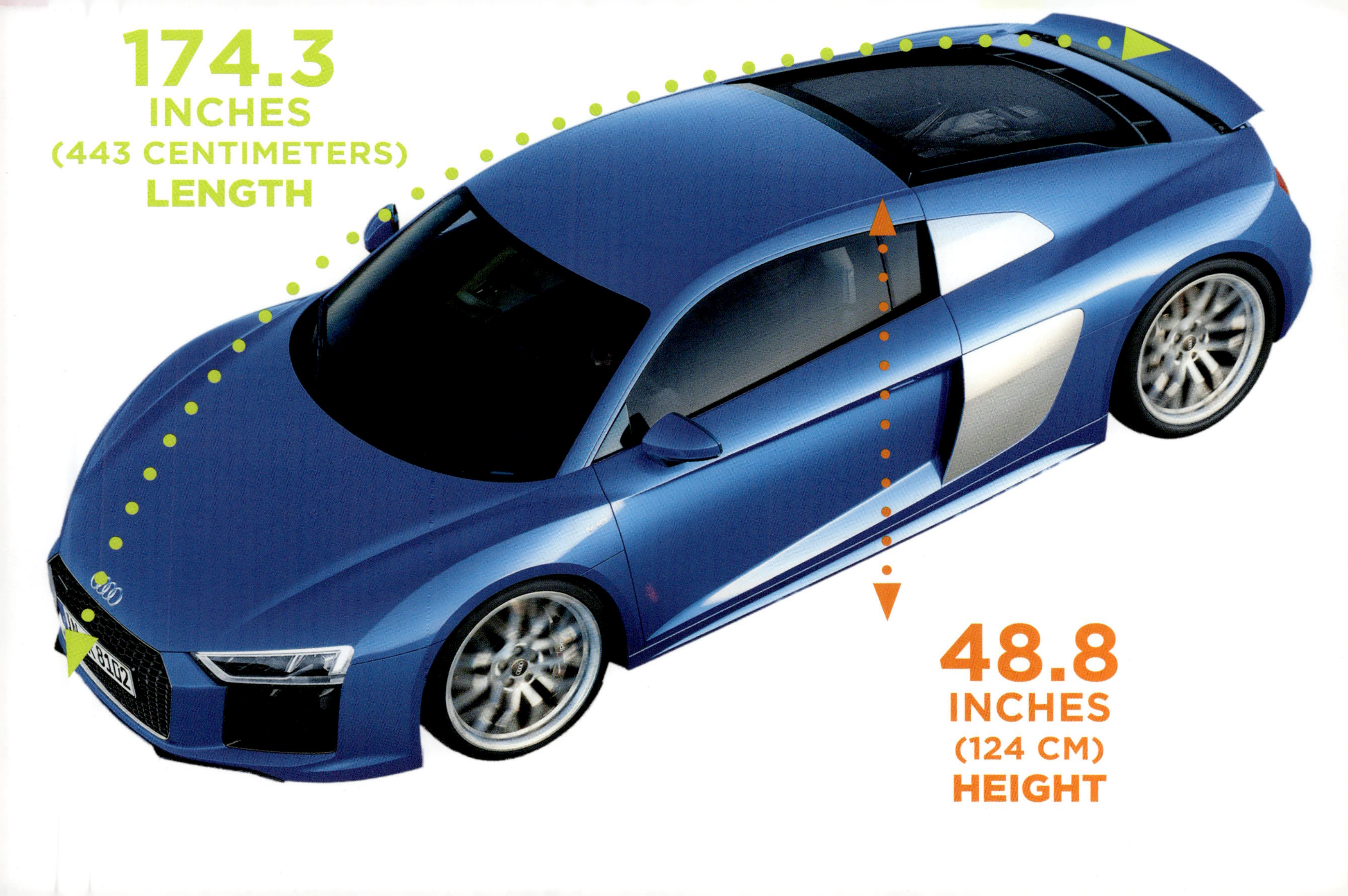
174.3
INCHES
(443 CENTIMETERS)
LENGTH
48.8
INCHES
(124 CM)
HEIGHT

CHAPTER 4

An Epic Car

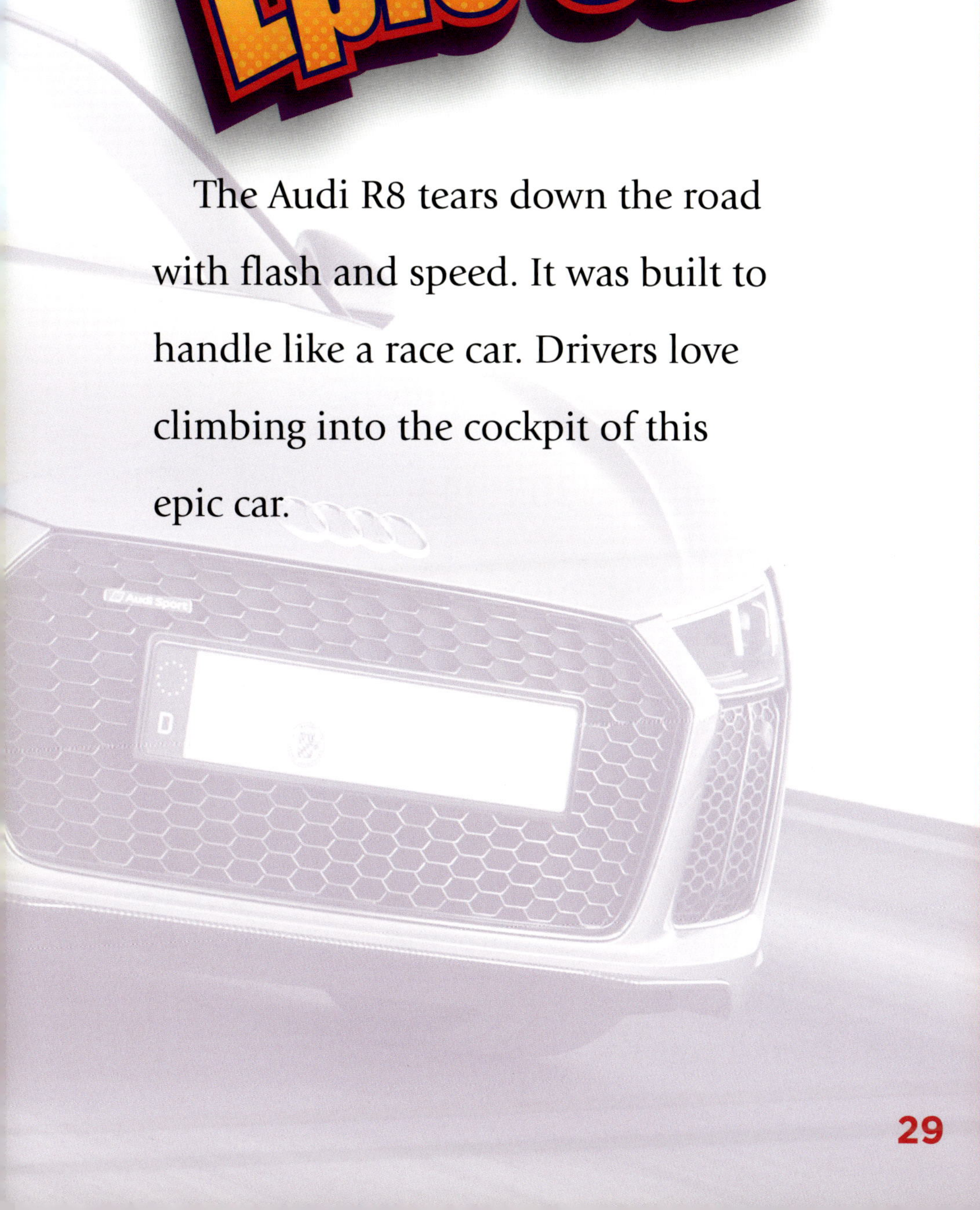

The Audi R8 tears down the road with flash and speed. It was built to handle like a race car. Drivers love climbing into the cockpit of this epic car.

aerodynamic (air-oh-dahy-NAM-ik)—something that is shaped so it moves easily through air

carbon fiber (KAR-buhn FAHY-bur)—a very strong, lightweight material

customize (KUS-tuh-myz)—to build, fit, or change according to individual specifications

drag (DRAYG)—something that makes action or progress slower or more difficult

gauge (GAYJ)—an instrument for measuring something

magnetic (mag-NEH-tik)—acting like a magnet

mileage (MAHY-lij)—the average number of miles a vehicle will travel on a gallon of gasoline

shock absorber (SHAHK ub-ZORB-ur)—a device connected to a vehicle's wheel in order to reduce the effect of bumps

suspension (suh-SPEN-shuhn)—the system of springs that supports the upper part of a vehicle on the axles

unveil (un-VAYL)—to make public

LEARN MORE

BOOKS

Fishman, Jon M. *Cool Sports Cars*. Awesome Rides. Minneapolis: Lerner Publications, 2019.

Mason, Paul. *German Supercars: Porsche, Audi, Mercedes.* Supercars. New York: PowerKids Press, 2019.

Sommer, Nathan. *Audi R8 Spyder.* Car Crazy. Minneapolis: Bellwether Media, Inc., 2020.

WEBSITES

2020 Audi R8 Coupe
www.audiusa.com/models/audi-r8

2020 Audi R8 Review, Pricing, and Specs
www.caranddriver.com/audi/r8

INDEX

B

body design, 4, 8–9, 10, 13, 27

C

colors, 18

costs, 6–7, 26

D

driving modes, 24, 25

I

interior design, 14, 16–17, 18

S

shock absorbers, 22

speed, 4, 20–21, 22

W

wheels, 18